NEW ORLEANS

Court of the Palm, on Royal Street, was built about 1812 by Dr. Raymond Devéze. The large palm in the center has grown to fit the enclosure and completely shades the court. The old stone drainage trough, the large rectangular flagstones, the wrought iron chandelier and the decorative cast iron on the wall, used partly to reinforce it, make this one of the most charming of all the courts.

NEW ORLEANS

STUART M. LYNN

AMERICAN LEGACY PRESS
NEW YORK

This 1982 edition is published by American Legacy Press,
distributed by Crown Publishers, Inc.
by arrangement with Hastings House Publishers, Inc.

Manufactured in the United States of America

Library of Congress Cataloging in Publication Data

Lynn, Stuart M.
New Orleans.

Reprint. Originally published: New York: Hastings
House, 1949.
Includes index.
1. New Orleans (La).—Buildings—Pictorial works.
2. Architecture—Louisiana—New Orleans—Pictorial works.
3. Decoration and ornament, Architectural—Louisiana—
New Orleans—Pictorial works. 4. Gardens—Louisiana—
New Orleans—Pictorial works. I. Title.
NA735.N4L9   1982   720'.9763'35   82-6648
                                          AACR2

ISBN: 0-517-011654
r q p o n m l k

CONTENTS

NEW ORLEANS

PREFACE

The city of New Orleans probably has more to offer photographically than any other city in our country; yet, with one or two exceptions, it has been virtually neglected by the camera. That no serious attempt has been made to present all its aspects and moods in a single volume is difficult to understand.

I came to New Orleans in the fall of 1938. It was love at first sight. I was fascinated with the delicate ironwork, the architecture, and the gay life of the people. To me it was different in still another way — there was a certain mood, a melancholia surrounding it, a sort of spell which came unconsciously from the dark still bayous, the moss-covered oaks, the white of magnolias against dark green foliage, the old cemeteries, the luxuriant growth, and the great river crawling to the Gulf. I looked at it once and went to work.

Since then I have been working toward the realization of a New Orleans portfolio. From the beginning my idea has been to gather from the vast wealth of photogenic material at hand a selection of prints representative of the city as a whole — a graphic record which would interest not only the tourist but also the architect, the ironworker, and the curator.

It has been a slow collection. To start with, Sunday has been the only day which could be devoted to the task. The war and material shortages delayed work for the better part of five years. Many Sundays were lost because of the subtropical rainfall. Many hours were spent waiting for the sun to come around, parked cars to move, tourists to pass, trying to find a certain courtyard gate unlocked or awaiting the arrival of spring when the courtyards and patios are most picturesque. But slowly, one by one, the negatives found their way into the file.

The illustrations appear in four groups. The first deals with architecture, the second with courtyards and patios, the third with ironwork, and the fourth with the city's fascinating old cemeteries. In each section the photographs have been arranged, as near as pos-

1

sible, in their proper location sequence. All the ironwork and tombs of each cemetery have been grouped together.

A better appreciation and understanding of the photographs can be gained by a thumbnail sketch of the city, its background and its present status.

The main thoroughfare Canal Street, at one time an open canal, divides the city into two distinctly different parts. Up river from it is referred to as "uptown" — the new section — and down river from it is "downtown" — the old section. Starting at the river and ending fifty blocks away in a jumble of old cemeteries, the great 171-foot-wide boulevard is more than a dividing line for the old and the new. It is a sort of fusion of the two which offers a separate and distinct flavor strongly reminiscent of South America. The buildings on either side are predominantly white. The sidewalks (known locally as *banquettes*) are of terrazzo design as is the center section, which easily accommodates four streetcar lines side by side. This is the shopping center and the main stage for the mirth and madness of Mardi Gras.

Uptown New Orleans resembles more the average American city. Here are the business and financial districts, the better homes and the universities. Its main artery is St. Charles Avenue, which curves gently for eighty blocks with the great crescent of the river. On the downtown side of Canal Street is the *Vieux Carré* or Old Square, generally referred to as the French Quarter. It is to New Orleans what the Montmartre is to Paris, what the Casbah is to Algiers. A maze of ancient and lovely architecture, it stands today, little changed by the years, the greatest outdoor show in America.

It is filled with fine restaurants, exquisite grillwork, carriage entrances mellow with age leading back to sunny courtyards, narrow, musty tunnelways opening into flowered patios, flagstoned alleys, countless antique shops, book stores, art dealers, quaint bars, bearded artists. And through it all are the smells of age, of roasting coffee and cooking pralines, the sounds of French and Italian spoken behind latticed doors, the clip-clop of shod feet, the fruit vendors calling from the streets and in winter, the coal man crying from his wagon: "Coal man coal, Coal man coal."

There has always been some degree of enmity between the old

and the new, an almost inevitable circumstance where there is a dividing line. Following the Louisiana Purchase, the French and Spanish settlers received the Americans with little or no enthusiasm. There was much confusion and misunderstanding due to the new language, customs and government which naturally became rapidly predominant. This diminished as resulting circumstances of disease and war forced a common cause. But as the Americans crossed Canal Street and began to build upriver, an unofficial severance took place with the old city extending one way and the new the other. Even the streets changed their names when they crossed Canal Street.

This feeling has persisted through the years. Many of the uptowners lost sight of the Quarter's true importance, its worth as an advertising agent, its unique character among American cities and the fact that with each passing year its value increased as an outdoor museum.

This indifference on the part of the majority reached its peak about 1909, when the city authorities leveled the 400 block between Royal and Chartres Streets, destroying its quaint and irreplaceable buildings, and erected the Civil Courts Building, which stands today out of place and out of tune with its surroundings, a monument to poor judgment. This, coupled with the destruction by fire of the old French Opera House in 1919 and the dismantling of the old St. Louis Hotel in 1915, constitutes the major loss of the French Quarter.

Today, however, the Quarter has changed somewhat. The years just prior to World War II might be called its renaissance period. The people began to see in it something more than a place for night life and good food. Many of the old buildings were renovated into apartments and homes. Much of the rowdyism vanished and tourists flocked in ever increasing numbers.

In fact, the whole city is changing. It seems to be more aware of its potentialities and its responsibilities than ever before. The stress is on international trade, especially with Central and South America, and another era, more golden than the steamboat era of 1830-1860, seems almost a reality.

S. M. L.

3

ARCHITECTURE

The buildings of the French Quarter were constructed mostly of brick, plaster, and cypress. The older ones are of a rather soft, locally-made brick laid between reinforcements of selected cypress timbers and plastered over to keep the damp subtropical climate from damaging them. This type of construction is known as *briqueté entre poteaux* or brick between posts. The plaster was usually painted in soft colors.

The roofs were either of cypress shingles or tile. However, after the disastrous fires of 1788 and 1794, brick and tile construction became compulsory. Lafitte's old blacksmith shop on page 51 is an excellent example of soft brick and tile construction.

The larger mansions were built from two to four stories high with shops on the ground floor and living quarters above. Large cypress doors open to the tunnel-like corridors that lead back to the courtyards. Along the sides of these courtyards were the slave quarters and to the rear were stables and carriage houses. Much pride was taken in the circular stairways, fan windows, and graceful arches.

Uptown in the garden district, beginning about 1830, the homes began to lean more and more toward Greek and Roman architecture. This influence, together with the natural inheritance of ornamental ironwork and brick-plaster construction, forms a composite architecture which belongs wholly to New Orleans. These homes are of two main types: the raised cottage and the two-story house. The main floor or living quarters of the raised cottage was built six or eight feet above the ground on an elevated foundation which served as a basement. The first floor of the two-story house was elevated three or four feet, these elevations being a safeguard against dampness. Both types had large gardens enclosed within cast iron fences or brick walls and usually gabled roofs with enough pitch to afford a half story of extra living space.

The Upper Pontalba Building faces its twin, the lower Pontalba, across Jackson Square. Both buildings were erected by the Baroness de Pontalba, daughter of Don Andres Almonester y Roxas, and designed by James Gallier, Sr., famous architect of the time. They are said to be the first apartment buildings in America. This building, completed in 1850, is now owned by the city government.

The cast-iron grillwork on both buildings was made in France and each panel contains the initials A P for Almonester and Pontalba.

Approximately 15 miles of docks help make New Orleans the second ranking ocean port in the United States. Much of its cargo consists of cotton, coffee, grain, bananas, sugar, and molasses. This view is from the bridge of the sight-seeing steamer "President," looking down river across the Canal Street Ferry landing.

Canal Street and the financial center as seen from a point near the custom-house.

The "*Marble Hall*" is the main business room of the Customhouse, 423 Canal Street. Built almost entirely of marble and supported by 14 massive Greek Corinthian columns it is one of the most impressive rooms in America. It measures 128 feet long by 84 feet wide with a height of 58 feet.

Godchaux Building at the corner of Canal and Chartres Streets was built about 1890 by Leon Godchaux, Sr., a merchant and plantation owner who specialized in the growing of sugar cane. The ground floor housed the Godchaux Clothing Store, now located at 828 Canal Street, and the upper stories were used then, as they are today, for offices. The building is typical of early Canal Street architecture.

11

Corner of Canal and St. Charles Streets looking toward the financial district. The old building in the foreground is the original "Crescent Billiard Hall," a century old gambling house. Of typical old New Orleans architecture, it has been a landmark on Canal Street for 125 years.

On the base of the lamp post can be seen one of the four plaques commemorating the French, Spanish, Confederate, and American dominations of the city.

Canal and Carondelet Streets. The old building on the right, constructed about 1882 and demolished in 1948, was originally the Pickwick Club, the scene of some of the most lavish balls in the city's history and, like the Crescent Billiard Hall and the old Godchaux Building, was typical of early Canal Street architecture. The Hibernia Bank colonade rises in the center background.

Royal Street. This view, taken from the lawn of the Civil Courts Building, shows many of the fine old buildings in the 400 and 500 blocks of the Quarter's main thoroughfare.

Old Absinthe House at the corner of Bourbon and Bienville Streets was built in 1806 by Pedro Font and Francisco Juncadella, importers of food and liquor. Later, as a bar, it acquired its name through the skill of Cayetano Ferrer in mixing an "Absinthe Frappe." One of the unique buildings of the Quarter, it has a secret floor between the two stories, which is another of the several places where General Jackson and Lafitte are supposed to have planned the Battle of New Orleans.

The Lights at Arnaud's, 811-13 Bienville Street. The restaurant was established in 1921 by the late Arnaud Cazenave, known affectionately as Count Arnaud. It soon gained a reputation which placed it among the select eating places of the city. The row of lights extend the whole length of the block. The building was erected in 1833.

Manheim's Antique Shop, 403 Royal Street, was built in 1821 as the Louisiana State Bank. The wrought iron initials L.S.B. can still be seen on the balcony railing. It was designed by Benjamin Henry Boneval Latrobe, who also designed the south wing of the Capitol Building in Washington, D. C. Before construction could be started, Latrobe died of yellow fever and it was completed by Benjamin F. Fox.

17

Antique Shop, 403 Royal Street. Displays like this stop thousands of tourists each year.

The Fencing Masters' Houses, corner of Conti Street and Exchange Alley. There had been sword play in New Orleans from the city's beginning, but during the golden era, from 1830 to 1860, dueling reached the height of its popularity. During this period the best known fencers opened academies to which the reckless youngbloods flocked.

The Patio Royal, 417 Royal Street, was built about 1802 by Don José Faurie, a wealthy Spanish merchant. It was purchased from him by the newly organized Louisiana Bank in 1805. In 1820 it was bought by Martin Gordon, close friend of Andrew Jackson. In 1841 it became the property of Judge Alonzo Morphy, father of Paul Charles Morphy, the famous chess player. The younger Morphy lived here for nearly forty years. In 1920, through the generosity of William Ratcliff Irby, the title passed to Tulane University. It is now an excellent French Restaurant. The double stairway leading from the corridor to the second floor is of unusual interest.

Antoine's Restaurant, 713 St. Louis Street, one of America's most famous eating places, was founded by Antoine Alciatore, who came to New Orleans in 1840 from Marseilles, France. After his death a son, Jules, took over the establishment. Today it is operated by Roy Alciatore, a grandson.

Such famous dishes as oysters Rockefeller and *pompano en papillote* were originated here. Through the years there has been little change in the building itself or in the methods of serving.

Lafcadio Hearn's Boarding House, 516 Bourbon Street, was built about 1827. Here, in a rented room, the myopic Hearn toiled ceaselessly over some of the esthetic pages that earned for him the title of "The Word Jeweler."

Napoleon House at 500 Chartres Street was built prior to 1798. It was the home of Mayor Nicolas Girod, who is supposed to have headed a plan to rescue Napoleon from St. Helena and bring him to New Orleans. If successful, the Mayor's home was to be placed at the disposal of the exile.

Court of the Three Arches Slave Quarters, 633 Toulouse Street, was built in 1825 by Dr. Germain Ducatel and designed by Benjamin F. Fox. Instead of the usual ironwork the balcony railings are of cypress. It is now used as an apartment house.

Fighting French Headquarters, 633 Royal Street, was at one time the first equivalent to the modern 5 and 10¢ store. In those days the picayune, 6¼¢, and the quartee, 2½¢, were in use. The building has also served as a Chinese laundry and a book bindery. It is now used in French relief work.

'Sieur George's House, at the corner of Royal and St. Peter Streets, is also known as the "skyscraper building" and Dr. Le Monnier's Home. Built by Dr. Yves Le Monnier, a physician, in 1811, it was called the skyscraper building because it was the first building erected in the Quarter with more than two stories. 'Sieur George, a fictional character in one of George W. Cable's stories, lived here.

Labranche Building, at the corner of Royal and St. Peter Streets, was built around 1835 by Jean Baptiste LaBranche, a wealthy sugar planter. Its cast-iron grillwork, of oak leaf and acorn design, is one of the finest examples in the French Quarter.

Orleans' Alley, better known to tourists and natives as "Pirate's Alley," runs along the south side of the Cathedral and St. Anthony's Garden. It is the scene of the outdoor art exhibit held each year during the Spring Fiesta.

Cabildo Alley, looking toward St. Peter Street. This alley, only one-half block in length, connects Pirate's Alley with St. Peter Street. Of the two buildings facing the camera the higher one to the left is Le Petit Salon, owned by an exclusive women's organization formed to preserve the traditions and culture of the Vieux Carré. The one to the right is known as O'Hara's Snuff Factory.

29

Mardi Gras, 1946. Rex, King of the Carnival and Lord of Misrule, pauses in front of the Boston Club on Canal Street to toast his queen with champagne.

Mardi Gras in Louisiana dates back to 1699, when Iberville came up the Mississippi River. Masquerade balls were first authorized by law in 1827 and street masking came about 1835. Parades were first held in Mobile. The first New Orleans parade was in 1838, after which they became organized events.

Mardi Gras (French, *Fat Tuesday*) is on Shrove Tuesday, which is followed by Ash Wednesday, the beginning of Lent. Shrove Tuesday is forty days, not counting Sundays, before Easter.

The Carnival season begins shortly after New Years and is celebrated with a series of dazzling parties, receptions, and balls until the beginning of Lent. During the final week the Carnival reaches a fervid tempo with parades, staged by the larger organizations, traveling for miles through the streets. The merrymaking reaches its peak on Mardi Gras day, when the people of the city, together with thousands of visitors, don costumes and masks and New Orleans becomes the "City that care forgot."

The largest parades are those of Momus, God of Mockery; Hermes, God of Commerce; Nor (New Orleans Romance) which is given by the school children of the city; Proteus, God of the Sea; Zulu, King of the Africans — the Negro burlesque of Rex; Rex, King of the Carnival and Lord of Misrule, and Comus, God of Mirth.

The Art Exhibit, in Pirate's Alley. Each year during the Spring Fiesta a day is set aside for the artists of Louisiana and the surrounding area to exhibit their work.

Old Spanish Arsenal, 615 St. Peter Street, is now the State Museum of War or Battle Abbey. Built in 1839 during the administration of Governor A. B. Roman, it was converted into a museum in 1915. It occupies the site of the old Spanish prison (Calabozo) which was built in 1769.

600 Block St. Peter Street. These high-balconied buildings, often referred to as "the heart of the Vieux Carré," are viewed from the Little Theatre looking toward Royal Street.

The Lower Pontalba Building, facing Jackson Square, is a twin to the upper
Pontalba (see page 7) and was completed in 1851. The building was recently
purchased by William Ratcliff Irby and donated to the Louisiana State
Museum.

Cabildo, Cathedral and Presbytere. As one faces the Cathedral the Cabildo is
to his left and the Presbytere to his right.

The Cabildo, the third building to occupy the site, was erected in 1795
by Don Andres Almonester y Roxas as a Capitol House for the legislative
assembly of the Spanish Colonial Government, the Very Illustrious Cabildo.
During the 20-day rule of the French in 1803 it was called the *Hotel de ville*
or City Hall. Originally, there was a balustrade on top, but in 1847 the
mansard roof was added. After the Louisiana Purchase, the Royal Arms of
Spain were removed from the pediment and replaced with the American
Eagle. The Cabildo was the scene, in 1803, of the transfer of Louisiana from

Spain to France and 20 days later from France to the U. S. Today it houses the historical and art sections of the Louisiana State Museum.

Don Almonester built the first story of the Casa Curial, now known as the Presbytere — the French word for the residence of a priest — just prior to the fire of 1794 which destroyed the building on the opposite side of the Cathedral. Since it was necessary to have a Capitol House, work on the Presbytere was halted in order to erect the Cabildo. The Presbytere was completed by the American Government about 1813. The mansard roof was added later to match that on the Cabildo. At present the building is owned by the Louisiana State Museum and houses the natural history exhibit.

St. Louis Cathedral, facing Jackson Square and the river, is the third church named after the patron Saint of Bourbon, France. The first was destroyed by a hurricane in 1722 and the second by fire in 1788. The present structure, built by Don Almonester y Roxas, was completed in 1794 but has since received several additions and alterations.

The bronze statue of General Andrew Jackson is the work of Clark Mills, a noted sculptor of the time. Its erection was proposed by the Baroness de Pontalba, who also financed most of the construction.

General Jackson returned to New Orleans in 1840 to lay the cornerstone of his monument, which was not completed until after the General's death. The inscription, "The Union Must and Shall Be Preserved," was ordered cut into the granite base by General Benjamin F. Butler, the Union Commander who occupied the city during the Civil War. The perfect balance of the horse, attained without the aid of props, is a feature which attracts much attention.

Cabildo and Cathedral from the side. This view is from Chartres and Wilkinson Streets. The balconies of the upper Pontalba Building are on the right.

St. Louis Cathedral from the rear, looking across St. Anthony's Garden. To the left is the building at 717 Orleans Street known as the Orleans Ballroom, supposedly the scene of the muchly publicized quadroon balls, which are now believed to have been held elsewhere.

The old and the new. This is a view of downtown New Orleans as seen through the third story grillwork of the old LePrète Mansion, now the New Orleans Academy of Art.

Le Prète Mansion, at the corner of Orleans and Dauphine Streets, was built by Dr. Joseph Coulon Gardette in 1835. Four years later it was sold to Jean Baptiste Le Prète, a prominent New Orleans merchant. It is noted for its cast-iron grillwork and high basement. Today it houses the New Orleans Academy of Art.

An interesting story concerning the mansion is told by Helen Pitkin Schertz in her "Legends of Louisiana." A Turk, known as the brother of the Sultan, so the tale goes, lived here for a short time in great secrecy with a bevy of beautiful girls until the officers and crew of their ship, at anchor on the riverfront, murdered the Turk and his girls, looted their house and made off to sea.

Maison Montegut, 731 Royal Street, was built prior to 1799. Of Spanish architecture, it has a spacious courtyard in the rear and wrought-iron bars protecting the show windows of the two antique shops on either side of the main entrance.

Madison Street, only one block long, extends from the French Market to Chartres Street.

The French Market, Decatur Street, was first erected in 1791 by the Spanish. Following destruction by a hurricane in 1812, it was rebuilt in 1813. In 1937-38 the market was completely modernized. It consists of three main branches, the meat and fish market, the fruit and vegetable market, and the farmers' market. Located at each end of the market are the Morning Call and the Café Dumond, famous coffee stands. Here, people of all classes come at all hours to *drink café noir* or *café au lait* and munch sugared doughnuts.

This view shows the Morning Call to the left, the fruit and vegetable market in the center and the meat and fish market to the right. The farmers' market, which is back to the left, cannot be seen in this photograph.

French Market Interior shows the fruit and vegetables ready for sale. Most of the stalls are operated by Italians.

Monteleone Bros. Banana Market, 95-7 French Market Place, is situated just behind the old United States Mint on what used to be tough, rowdy Gallatin Street. It faces the farmers' market and does a thriving business in fruits and produce. Today the building has lost most of its charm through remodeling. This view was taken in 1939.

The 1100 Block of Decatur Street is the Italian district next to the French Market.

The Miltenberger Home, corner Royal & Dumaine Streets, was built in 1839 by the widow of Dr. Christian Miltenberger, who served as surgeon in the Battle of New Orleans. Its extensive cast-iron balconies are of the oak leaf and acorn design.

600 Block Dumaine Street, looking from Chartres Street toward Royal, is full of quaint buildings and patios. The tall buildings at the far end are the old Miltenberger Homes.

Madame John's Legacy at 628 Dumaine Street was supposedly built by Jean Pascal, a French sea captain, about 1728. This would make it the oldest house in the Mississippi Valley. It is of the raised cottage type and takes its name from one of the characters in George W. Cable's story *'Tite Poulette*. Today it belongs to the Louisiana State Museum.

Jean Lafitte's Blacksmith Shop, at the corner of Bourbon and St. Philip Streets, was built prior to 1772. The house was supposedly used by the Lafitte Brothers as a smithy in order to appear as respectable as possible while carrying on their real business of piracy and smuggling. Note the diagonal placing of handhewn timber in the brick, a type of architecture known as "*briqueté entre poteaux*" or brick between posts. The building now serves as a bar and restaurant.

The Silo Court, 1015 Chartres Street. The silo-like construction at the center houses the stairway. Of unusual interest are its three landings serving a two story house.

The Beauregard House, 1113 Chartres Street, was built in 1827 by Joseph Le Carpentier, grandfather of Paul Charles Morphy. The latter was born in the house in 1837 and later became one of the great chess masters of the world. It is now a memorial to General P. G. T. Beauregard, "the great Creole," Louisiana Confederate leader who lived there at one time.

The Ursuline Convent, 1114 Chartres Street, is, perhaps, the second oldest building in the Mississippi Valley. Construction was begun in 1730 and completed in 1734.

The Ursuline nuns came to New Orleans in 1727, the first of their order to establish themselves in America. During the past two centuries it has been used as a convent for girls, a school for Indians, a palace for the Archbishop of the Diocese, a meeting place for the Louisiana Legislature, an academy for boys and now as a Presbytery to St. Mary's Italian Church which it now joins.

The Charity Hospital of New Orleans, 1532 Tulane Avenue, is operated by the State of Louisiana for its needy citizens. The twenty-story building, completed in 1939, is one of the largest hospitals in America. The Tulane University Medical School (Hutchinson Memorial Building) is to the left. The larger building to the right is the Louisiana State University Medical School. Both Universities train their students at the hospital. The doctors of New Orleans give a certain amount of their time each week to the institution.

The City Hall, 543 St. Charles Avenue, faces Lafayette Square. It was designed and built by James Gallier, Sr. in 1850 and is considered one of the finest examples of Greek Ionic architecture in the country.

The City Hall Pediment with figures cut in high relief represents Liberty, Justice, and Commerce.

St. Charles Street from Lafayette Square. The building with the cast iron balconies on the right belongs to the Choctaw Club, a political organization whose name is derived from the Choctaw Indians of Louisiana. The hotel grill-work is at the corner of Poydras Street. The Masonic Temple Building towers above it.

In the Center of Lee Circle, from the top of the 60-foot marble, Doric column, the 16½-foot bronze statue of General Robert E. Lee looks down St. Charles Street to the business district. The memorial was dedicated in 1884 on Washington's birthday.

Entrance to the Charles F. Buck, Jr. residence at 2027 Carondelet Street, has pilasters with composite capitals, modillioned cornice, and rich mouldings. The cast iron incorporates a floral design to match the carved flowers on the door. The panes around the door are of Bohemian etched glass.

Maginnis Home, 2127 Prytania Street. A fine example of the raised cottage house with excellent corinthian columns, ironwork, and cornice. The house was presented to the New Orleans Chapter of the American Red Cross in 1939 by Mrs. George Rose, who was Josephine Maginnis.

The Forsyth House, 1134 First Street. Jefferson Davis, first and only President of the Confederacy, died here in 1889. It is a typical two story house with Greek Ionic columns below and Egyptian-like Corinthian above. At the time of President Davis' death the house was owned by his intimate friend, Judge Charles Erasmus Fenner.

The James House, 2405 Prytania Street. Built before the Civil War, it is noted for its ironwork on the exterior and its woodwork on the interior. It is now an apartment house.

The Robert L. Perkins Home, 2702 St. Charles Avenue, was built about 1857 by a sea captain. The architecture was probably influenced by the steamboat era. The house is square with the first and fourth stories smaller than the second and third. A spiral stairway leads from the ground floor to the belvedere from which, with the aid of a spy glass, the captain observed ship movements on the river. For many years a duplicate of the house stood on the next lot.

2728 St. Charles Avenue. This old home is about one hundred years old. It was converted from a raised cottage to the present columned mansion.

The Freret Mansion, 1525 Louisiana Avenue, was built in 1857 by James P. Freret as a plantation home on the then suburban avenue. It has 22 rooms.

The Orleans Club, 5005 St. Charles Avenue, was built in 1868. In 1925 it was purchased and remodeled by an exclusive New Orleans Women's Club.

The Howard Tilton Memorial Library of Tulane University, completed in 1941, contains over 250,000 volumes. The Lafcadio Hearn room on the first floor is of especial interest.

Wrought-iron gates form the entrance to the Administration Building of Newcomb College, 1229 Broadway. Newcomb, a school for women, is affiliated with Tulane University.

The Huey P. Long Bridge crosses the Mississippi River at a point about 10 miles above New Orleans and links the city with Texas and the West. Of cantilever and truss construction, it was completed in 1935 at a cost of $13,000,000. It accommodates railway, automotive, and pedestrian traffic. Counting its railway approaches, the bridge is 4.4 miles long. It measures 409 feet from the base of foundation to the top of superstructure, and allows ships a clearance of approximately 150 feet at normal river level.

No treatment of New Orleans architecture is complete without some mention of the fabulous plantation houses nearby.

Prior to the Civil War the vast plantation tracts were, with the aid of slave labor, producing the wealth and prestige of Louisiana's golden era. During this time the plantation house became the symbol of success. They went up all along the banks of the Mississippi and the bayous with each landowner trying to outdo the other.

Today many of these structures are still standing. Some of them are in use and, sad to relate, some have reached a state of decay beyond which there is no salvage.

Ashland and Belle Grove were two of the largest and finest to be built. Today they are great hulking ghosts facing each other across the Mississippi.

Ashland was designed by Gallier and built by Duncan Kenner in 1841. Situated above the town of Geismar, La., it is the most impressive house still standing on the east bank of the river. Surrounded by 28 square pillars it sits far back from the levee in a grove of moss covered live oaks. The massive entablature, the great square pillars and the low roof create an impression of mass and weight. The house was called Ashland after the Kentucky home of Henry Clay whom Kenner, also a politician, greatly admired. Duncan Kenner was also a great sportsman. He bred his own running horses, maintained a private race track, and promoted racing among the plantation owners.

After the Civil War, Kenner regained Ashland and some of his wealth. Following his death the new owner changed the name of the house to Belle Helene; but it had lost much of its former glamor and prestige and by the turn of the century Ashland was on its way down.

Belle Grove is on the west bank of the river a few miles below White Castle, La. Built in 1857 by John Andrews, a Virginian, it was the largest and probably the most beautiful of all the plantation houses.

Like Ashland it was designed by Gallier. Despite the formal dignity that marks the place there is something friendly and inviting about the classic sweep of the marble steps ascending to the porch between heavy blocks of plastered brick. The columns and pilasters are splendid examples of the true Greek Corinthian order. Above them the immense entablature and pediment rest in lofty grandeur. The final count of rooms is said to have reached 75, which gave the Andrews plenty of room for their grand scale entertainment.

Shortly after the end of the Civil War, John Andrews sold Belle Grove to Henry Ware, who turned the place over to his son, James Ware. Like the Andrews, the Wares entertained lavishly. They built a race track. Their son Stone Ware built a second one. They had large weekend parties featured by days of racing during which the house overflowed with guests.

Suddenly all this was changed. The plantation suffered from storms and droughts which kept production at a minimum. Then the crops failed completely and in 1924 the glory of Belle Grove came to an end.

Today the pinkish cast of the house is faded and mildewed. The doors sag and the paneless windows are voids of ghostly black.

Chalmette Monument is a few miles below the city on the east bank of the Mississippi. It commemorates the Battle of New Orleans in 1815 and marks General Andrew Jackson's position during the fighting. Its construction, started in 1855, was interrupted by the Civil War and finished in 1908. It is 110 feet high.

Fort Macomb guarded the Chef Menteur, the smaller of two passes connecting Lake Borgne with Lake Pontchartrain. The Fort was built during the War of 1812 by Andrew Jackson. These are the gun chambers with some of the circular gun-tracks still intact.

Fort Pike was built to guard the Pass Rigolets, seen beyond the curve of the gun parapet. It was built just after the War of 1812 by Andrew Jackson. The two forts were constructed to guard against an invasion of New Orleans from Lake Pontchartrain.

COURTYARDS AND PATIOS

There is some confusion regarding the use of the words "courtyard" and "patio" and ofttimes the two are erroneously used interchangeably. Generally speaking, the courtyard, which is of French origin, is larger than the patio and bounded by high walls. It has a wide, flagstoned carriage entrance or corridor leading to it from the street. Some of the smaller courts are completely paved with flagstones while the larger ones may have grass plots, flower beds, large trees, fountains, and statues. The patio, on the other hand, is of Spanish origin and is a smaller, inner space more within the outer walls of the house, and has a small, narrow entrance along the side of or through the house itself. It is paved either with flagstones or brick and contains many potted plants and ornaments.

Many of these courtyards and patios are closed to the public so that the average tourist sees them only through the entrance grill. If there is no grill, the court beyond can be seen only in the early morning when the doors are opened by servants who water and sweep the flagstones, a common practice during the hot summer months.

Mysing's Court, 722 St. Louis Street, also known as the old Conand Mansion, was built about 1808 by Dr. Joseph Conand. It is closed to visitors but can be seen through the gateway grille.

Napoleon House Patio is now used in conjunction with the Napoleon House Bar.

Brulatour Court, formerly Seignouret Court, 520 Royal Street, was built in 1816 by François Seignouret of Bordeaux, France, a wine importer and furniture-maker of note. Later, from 1870-86, Pierre Ernest Brulatour, another wine importer, used the building. In 1900 it passed into the hands of William Ratcliff Irby. The entresol, or mezzanine, a half story just above the ground floor, was used to store the casks of wine.

Casa Merieult, 529 Royal Street, was built in 1792 by Jean François Merieult and was one of the few buildings which escaped the disastrous fire of 1794. The courtyard and buildings are in excellent repair. Its three Royal Street shops deal in antiques, rare prints, and books and attract a discriminating clientele.

Patio at 718 Toulouse Street. This is the patio to the rear part of the Casa Merieult, whose courtyard is shown on the preceding page. The patio and courtyard are connected by a short hallway.

Hotel Maison de Ville Patio, 727 Toulouse St. The building to this patio was erected in 1800 by Jean Babtiste Lille Sarpy. The gate at the far left leads to the Court of Two Sisters.

Court of the Two Lions, 710 Toulouse Street, was built in 1798 by Don Juan Francisco Merieult. It gains its name from the two lions couchant atop the gate posts. High above the court the balcony is enclosed with green shutters. The main building faces Royal Street.

The Court of the Three Arches, 635-37 Toulouse Street, is actually a patio separating the slave quarters from the main building which faces Royal Street.

Demarchy's Court and Stairway, 625 Toulouse Street. Jean Antoine Demarchy, well known builder of the early days, erected this building in 1807. The beautiful winding stairway has long been admired by tourists and artists alike.

Court of the Two Sisters, 613 Royal Street, was built in 1832. One of the most famous courtyards in the Quarter, it gained its name from the two Camor sisters, who operated a fancy and variety store in the building from 1886 to 1906. In 1947 the rear wall of the court was torn down to include the Bourbon Street patio beyond, making it the largest courtyard in the Quarter. At this time a cast iron trellis was erected near its center for the wistaria vine.

Courtyard of the Royal Castilian Arms, 628 Royal Street. The building was
erected about 1795 by Charles Loubies, a wealthy planter.

Pat O'Brien's Courtyard, 718 St. Peter Street. The building was formerly the Casa de Fléchier and was built about 1792 by Étienne Marie de Fléchier. Today it is one of the most beautiful and elaborate bars in the city.

Wood Whitesell's Patio and Studio, 726 St. Peter Street, was formerly Faisendieu's *Posada* or Tavern. Although it has the courtyard entrance it is in the nature of a patio and is generally referred to as such today. Mr. Whitesell, affectionately known as "Pop," has had his studio of photography and living quarters here for the past fifteen years.

Patio at 623 St. Peter Street. To the left is one of the most spic and span praline kitchens in the Quarter. Here, colored women in starched blue dresses and yellow tignons (large handkerchiefs tied about the head in turban fashion) make the delicious candy cakes. Adjacent is a restaurant which specializes in that most famous of New Orleans dishes—gumbo.

Patio of The Little Theatre, 616 St. Peter Street, as seen through one of its fanned doorways. The organization started in 1916 as the Drawing Room Players. After continued success and increased membership they built the present theater with a façade along the lines of the Old Absinthe House on Bourbon Street and a seating capacity of 500.

Bosque House Court at 619 Chartres Street was built by Bartolome Bosque, a prosperous Spanish merchant, in 1795. It was the home of Suzette Bosque, Governor Claiborne's third wife.

Old Spanish Courtyard at 532-34 Madison Street is another court seldom seen by tourists. Lyle Saxon, noted author of books on Louisiana, restored the house and lived here for a number of years before his death in 1946.

Entrance to the Daniel Clark Patio, 823 Royal Street. The old stairway has many charming irregularities. This was the home of Daniel Clark, an Irishman, who shot Governor Claiborne in the leg when challenged on the field of honor. It is also said that he was one of Jean Lafitte's secret agents. It is now the home of the painter, Alberta Kinsey.

Marchand Patio and Stair, 830 Royal Street, was built in 1808 by Salomon Prevost, an early lawyer, and later sold to Jean Baptiste Marchand. The quaint winding stairway of cypress is much admired by tourists and artists. The Marchand family still occupies the building.

Madame John's Patio Stairway leads to the slave quarters behind the main building, which, with its lower floor of brick and upper of wood, is at variance with the "town" houses that make up the rest of the quarter.

This courtyard, like many others, has recently been restored and the building around it converted into modern apartments.

Old Spanish Stables, 716-24 Governor Nicholls Street, were built in 1834 by Judge Gallien Préval as a commercial livery stable. It is commonly pointed out as the Spanish Cavalry Stables and Barracks although the Spanish soldiers had left the city many years before the stables were erected.

Courtyard of the Gauché Mansion, 704 Esplanade Avenue at Royal Street. The mansion, one of the most imposing buildings in the Quarter, was built by John Gauché in 1856. The building is also noted for its cast iron railings.

IRONWORK

With its European background it is only natural that ironwork should have flourished in New Orleans on a scale unprecedented in America. In the early days there was only wrought iron — iron wrought or hammered by hand over a forge and anvil. Although much of this early ironwork was made in New Orleans, most of the better examples were shipped from Spain. The Spanish iron contains very little carbon and resists rust to a remarkable degree. The oldest of this ironwork is but slightly pitted and seems to have worn away rather than rusted. If a piece of this old iron is sawed through, the cross section will show a grain similar to wood.

About 1830 cast iron became popular. It is poured molten into molds of desired form and design and allowed to harden. The names of many New Orleans foundries are found on cast ironwork but much of it came from the East, especially from Philadelphia. One such firm, Wood and Perot, made much of the cast ironwork in the cemeteries. Unlike wrought iron, cast iron is hard and brittle, contains more carbon, and rusts rather easily. For this reason it is always painted.

From an aesthetic viewpoint it is hard to choose between them. Certainly, both forms are extremely picturesque in effect. Wrought iron is delicate and graceful and, like anything made by hand, has a certain character and charm. Cast iron, although not so flowing in design, follows a definite pattern of lace work design that is very striking, and often covers the entire front and side of a corner building in contrast to the wrought iron which is used sparingly for railings, guards, and supports. Also, wrought iron usually portrays inanimate objects whereas cast iron leans more to animate forms.

The ironwork, which played such an important part in the ornamentation of the homes of the living, was transplanted to the cemeteries. Here, with additional and more exaggerated motifs, it took on an even greater importance. Many of the tombs are surrounded by iron fences whose gates are of especial significance since they carry a theme or motif in symbolic form. Beautiful wrought-iron crosses crown some of the earlier tombs and gates, and occasionally grave markers of heavy cast iron are to be found.

Today, ironwork is produced in New Orleans on a small scale and is rather expensive. The modern cast iron is an excellent reproduction of the older iron but the wrought iron has nothing of the character and beauty of the hammered work which graces the older balconies.

Before entering the sections devoted to ironwork and cemeteries something should be said of the motifs incorporated in these works of iron and stone and the meanings behind them.

In an endeavor to perpetuate ideas in some subtle form the use of symbols has always played an important part in funeral art. The roots of this art in New Orleans came naturally from Europe, were nourished by the appalling years of yellow fever and cholera, and thus reached a growth unparalleled in America.

Just as the cross has always been the symbol of Christianity, so we find the inverted torch the symbol for death, the dove for love and peace, fruit for plenty, the lyre for music, the weeping willow tree for sadness, the winged hour glass for flight of time, a cup for the Holy Grail, a lamb for innocence, an all seeing eye for God, a wreath for honor and esteem, and the cathedral arch for the church.

Many floral designs are cut in delicate relief on the stone work. Of these flowers the greatest repetition is of the rose, the lily of the valley, the morning glory, and the forget-me-not. Another influence seen in many of these designs is that of the sea. In the French Quarter the sea shell design in cast iron is common. In the cemeteries, beside the iron work pertaining to the sea, there is an old custom of whitewashing large conch shells and placing them on or near the tombs.

These symbols are used either singly or in conjunction with human forms in delineations which tell definite and pathetic stories.

Wrought Iron Balcony over Waldhorn's Antique Shop, 343 Royal Street, was erected in 1800 by Don Pablo Lanusse during the Spanish domination. This is probably the finest example of wrought iron in the city.

Balcony Supports on the Roquette Mansion, 413 Royal Street. Many of the older balconies are partly supported by ornamental wrought iron brackets. The initials, D R, on the railing stand for Domingue Roquette, the former owner and wine merchant.

Balcony Guard or *garde de frise* on balcony at 520 Royal Street. Of particular interest is the beautiful wrought iron S incorporated in the design, the initial of François Seignouret, who erected the building.

Morning Glory Grillwork, 821 Toulouse Street, is an example of extremely delicate cast iron. Usually the cast iron work is heavier and less ornate.

The Wishing Gates at the Spanish Arms Court, 616 Royal Street. The building was erected in 1831 by Dr. Isador Labatut. The heavy wrought-iron gates were removed from the old Masonic Temple at the time of its demolition and placed at the end of the corridor in 1931. They are a favorite subject for photographers, etchers and painters.

The Charm Gates in the Court of Two Sisters, 613 Royal Street. These gates are famous in the Vieux Carré and are a splendid example of wrought iron. A small sign on them reads: "Charm Gates. These gates are over 200 years old. Touch them they will give you charm." Note their resemblance to the gates on the next page.

Gate at 917 North Rampart Street. Of all the wrought iron gates in New Orleans these gates and the ones on the preceding page are the only ones that bear any strong resemblance to each other.

Close up view of the cast iron oak leaf and acorn design on the Labranche Building, corner Royal and St. Peter Streets. See page 27.

Wrought Iron and Shadows. These are the entrance gates to Wood White-sell's studio of photography at 726 St. Peter Street.

The Railing of the Violin Shop, Bourbon and St. Peter Streets. The display of violins adds a weird touch to this rather simple wrought iron railing of Cathedral-arch design.

Cabildo Wrought Iron and Fan Windows. The iron work on the front of the Cabildo is patterned from the rosette and crown designs.

A P Initials of Almonester and Pontalba on the cast-iron railings of the Pontalba buildings.

The Corn Stalk Gate, 915 Royal Street. The date of the erection of this gate is unknown but it is thought to have been shortly after 1830 when cast iron began to supplement wrought iron. Each gate post rests on a pumpkin and the stalks are entwined with morning glories. A large butterfly adorns the central part and the whole is painted in natural color.

117

The Balcony at Casa Correjolles, 715 Governor Nicholls Street, built by Gabriel Correjolles in 1834. In 1909 the house passed into the possession of Sherwood Anderson, the novelist. The lace work shadow above the railing is from ornamental ironwork on the eaves of the balcony roof.

Cast Iron Doorway Gates at the Old Spanish Customhouse, 1300 Moss Street, on Bayou St. John. Andrew Jackson and Jean Lafitte are supposed to have met in the original part of the house in regard to the defense of New Orleans. The gates are a later addition.

Gate of the Goddess Fortuna, 1533 Magazine Street, has a base of heavy medieval studding supporting a large rosette. At the top between two lyres adorned with grapes and framed in arabesques is the Roman Goddess Fortuna, resting one hand on an anchor and holding a cornucopia in the other in tribute to the great river and the vast wealth it was then bringing to New Orleans.

The Old Cartwright Eustis Home, 1410 Jackson Avenue, now houses Soulé College. This is a good example of Louisiana architecture incorporating both classic and Creole influences, with Ionic columns below, Corinthian above, and dentiled cornice. The cast-iron railings of lyre design are topped by swirls of wrought iron. The heavy cast fence is crowned with the beautiful antefix design.

Tomb of the Orleans Battalion of Artillery, St. Louis Cemetery No. 1. The Orleans Artillery took part in the War with Mexico. Each of the 16 vaults is sealed with heavy cast iron fronts. On each of these, standing out in bold relief are four cannon balls, two inverted torches, a wreath and the number of the vault. Above in the center of the pediment is the winged hourglass.

Urn and Arrow Gate, St. Louis Cemetery No. 2. This graceful little gate is a classic example of wrought iron beauty. The definite urn shape is also likened to a lyre with the arrows forming the strings. The design is seen again on a balcony railing in Toulouse Street, possibly indicating some connection between the occupants of the old house and the tomb.

Lyre Gate with Chalice, St. Louis Cemetery No. 2. The central idea of this gate was probably taken from the Holy Grail.

Winged Hourglass Gate, St. Louis Cemetery No. 2. This gate incorporates both wrought and cast iron. The motif of the winged hourglass could well have been designed from the thought expressed by so many great writers, "Art is long and time is fleeting: that is the tragedy of every great soul."

125

The Gate of Hearts, St. Louis Cemetery No. 2. The motif of hearts is beauti-
fully executed in graceful scrolls against the cold white of the marble.

Wrought Iron Cross on top of a tomb in St. Louis Cemetery No. 2. Many of the old tombs, especially in this cemetery, are crowned with similar crosses — all of wrought iron. Note the 12 scrolls in the fan and the clock hand pointing upward.

Lyre Gate, St. Louis Cemetery No. 3. This is one of the later examples of wrought iron and was made in New Orleans by G. C. Timpe, Camp Street.

Weeping Willow Gate, St. Louis Cemetery No. 3. Here a weeping willow tree, with doves above and lamps couchant beneath, reflects sorrow and innocence. Of cast iron it was made by Wood and Perot of Philadelphia.

Gothic Cathedral Design, St. Patrick's Cemetery No. 2. This heavy cast iron fence is an example of the ironwork which supplanted the more delicate wrought iron in the cemeteries. Note the conch shell.

Gate of the Kneeling Angel, St. Patrick's Cemetery No. 3, is an unusual piece of cast-iron work. The angel, kneeling before an incense altar, is particularly interesting because of her disproportionate body, with tiny hands and feet.

This unique arrangement of wrought and cast iron in Greenwood Cemetery
is strengthened by the contrast of sinister black with blinding white.

Iron Tombheads, Greenwood Cemetery. These twin tombheads of heavy cast iron are good examples of the ironworker's art. The upper halves are bordered with a delicate wreath of tendrils laden with fruit which surround an all-seeing eye and a mask surmounted by a dove's nest. Supporting these at the bases are two mermaid angels with crossed wings, the lower bodies terminating in beautiful scrolls.

Weeping Cupid Gate, Cypress Grove Cemetery. Since the gate is crowned with the lovebird design, it seems reasonable to assume that a love affair was interrupted by death leaving the little cupid distressed and weeping. Note the repetition of the inverted death torches, one of which cupid carries.

Flight of Time. This pagoda-like marker is found over a grave in Cypress Grove Cemetery. The motif of the winged hourglass (see also page 125) was probably a direct outgrowth of the yellow fever years when the span of life was often so short.

Modern Use of Ironwork I. Twin Stair Railing at 2607 Coliseum Street. Modern wrought-iron leading to the main entrance landing of a modern raised cottage — typical inheritance of the past.

Modern Use of Ironwork II. Gates of Modern Wrought Iron on upper St. Charles Avenue. This is probably the best example of modern wrought iron in the city. It is one of the few successful attempts to duplicate the material appearance and grace of the older work.

Modern Use of Ironwork III. Many of the city's modern homes are using small porches of cast iron similar to this one on State Street which makes an effective frame work for the beautiful door.

Modern Use of Ironwork IV. Doorway Gates and Balcony Railing in the Metairie Subdivision. All these designs are replicas of cast iron found in the Vieux Carré. The top panels of the gates are of the morning glory design The gates are framed with grapevines and the balcony railing is an exact duplicate of the railing on the two Pontalba buildings except for the absence of the A P initials.

CEMETERIES

Burial in New Orleans has always presented a problem since the ground level is lower than the river and barely higher than the surrounding swamps. The Catholic Religion, always predominant in the city, further complicated the problem by forbidding cremation. Interment in the water-soaked ground was practiced until about 1800, after which it became compulsory to build tombs above the ground. From this time on the cemeteries of New Orleans became famous.

The early tombs, like the early houses of the city, were built of brick and plaster and were usually painted white, causing an almost blinding glare in the summer sun. Some of them were built for one or two people, others for whole families. Small mausoleums, with as many as 60 or 70 vaults, were constructed to accommodate the members of various societies. Along the boundary lines of the cemeteries long walls of vaults are built in tiers usually four deep. These are referred to as "oven vaults."

In these old cemeteries there exists an architecture which stands alone and distinct from all other architectures. There is a direct simplicity to the shape of tombs, to their adornments and to the epitaphs which irresistibly carry one back to a day long gone, to a day when epidemics and plagues took a fearful toll and left the mind desperately preoccupied with death and its idealization.

In 1832 the death rate from yellow fever and Asiatic cholera reached staggering proportions. During a period of approximately three weeks more than one-sixth of the 36,000 people who remained in the city died — an average of about 300 a day, and in 1853 another epidemic of yellow fever took 8,000 in four months.

Knowing something of this background it is easy to perceive

how the emotional reaction of the people to their surroundings passed from profound thought into material forms, thus creating a strange and beautiful art in stone and iron and an irrepressible atmosphere of melancholy brooding.

Today the old cemeteries, though some are crumbling, are much the same as they were during the turbulent yesteryears and for those who are interested in them there are wonderful little discoveries at every turning.

The Dueling Oaks in City Park are included in the section on cemeteries because many of the encounters beneath them were preludes to the burial ground. The two great oaks stand close to the Delgado Art Museum on the bank of the City Park lagoon. The rectangular dueling mound rises gently midway between them. Many duels were fought here in the days before the Civil War and fatalities were common.

The last duel at the Oaks was fought as late as 1939 between two students from the Fencing Academy at 528 Royal Street. The encounter took place early one Sunday morning. The challenged man chose sabres and both contestants sustained severe cuts.

Louis Allard, former owner of the plantation that now forms City Park, is buried under the far tree.

Here also rests the body of
MICAJAH GREEN LEWIS
brother of Eliza W Claiborne
and private Secretary to Governor Claiborne
who fell in a duel
Feb.ry 14th 1805
in the 25th year of his age

Tomb of Micajah Green Lewis, who fell in a duel. This epitaph in St. Louis Cemetery No. 1 to Governor Claiborne's private secretary is one of the many reminders, found in the older cemeteries, of "coffee and pistols for two" beneath the oaks.

143

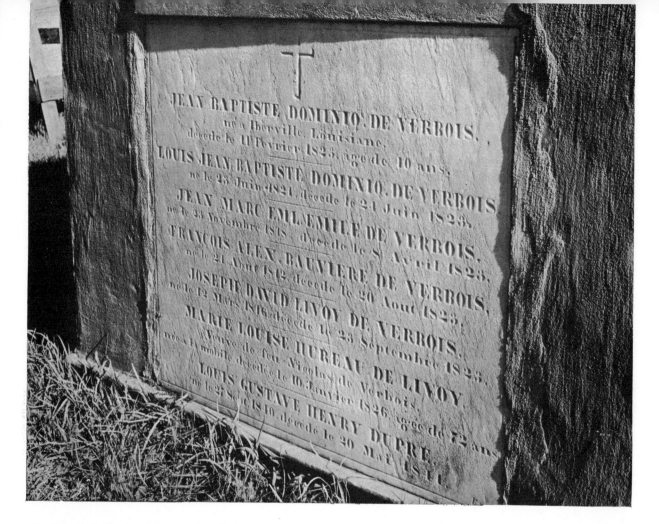

De Verbois Family Tomb, St. Louis Cemetery No. 1. The dates on this tomb show the appalling death rate from yellow fever. Of the seven names five of them died within seven months of the same year. The oldest of these was eleven years. Only one of the seven escaped an early death.

Tomb of Marie Laveau, the Voodoo queen, St. Louis Cemetery No. 1. Many weird tales are told about the voodoo queen of New Orleans, who dealt in charms and the feared *gris gris*. Robert Tallant in his book *Voodoo in New Orleans* tells of two Marie Laveaus, the second being the daughter of the first. It seems fairly certain that the first Marie was born about 1796 and died in

FAMILLE Vve PARIS
nee LAVEAU
Ci Git
MARIE PHILOME GLAPION.
décédée le 11 Juin 1897,
âgée de Soixante deux ans.
Elle fut bonne mère, bonne amie, et
regretté par tous ceux qui l'ont connue
Passants priez pour elle.

Cpe DUMENY DE GLAPION.
decede le 26 Juin 1855.
ARCANGE GLAPION.
decede le 6 Janvier 1845.
Jn EUGENE CROCKER.
decede le 5 Mai 1845.
ESMERALDA CROCKER.
decedee le 5 Janvier 1850.

1881. According to records, the second Marie was born in 1827 (according to the epitaph above 1835) and evidently died in the 1890's. However, it is certain that she (or they) held considerable power in the city.

The crosses on the face of the tomb were made with small pieces of red brick by her faithful followers and the many tourists who are told of the custom by guides.

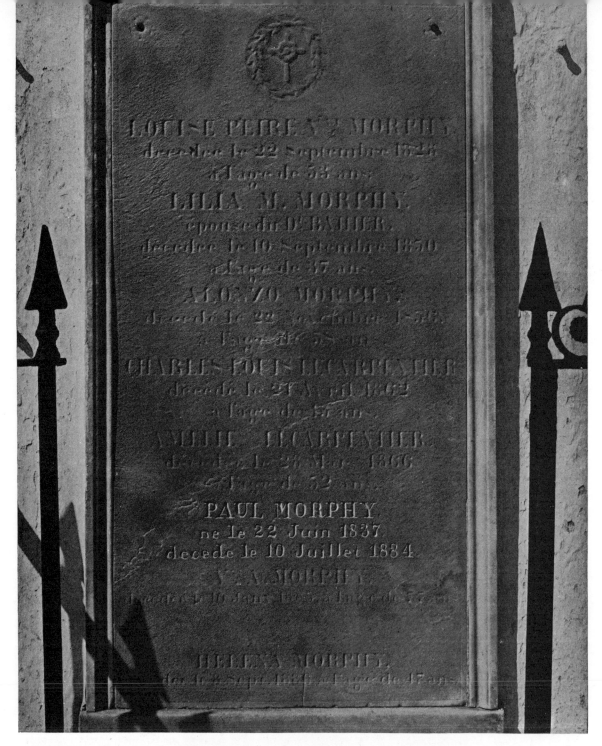

Paul Morphy's Tomb, St. Louis Cemetery No. 1. Time and the elements have reduced many of the older epitaphs to bare legibility. Many of the more famous names such as Paul Morphy's, one of the world's great chess players, have been rechiseled, mostly for the benefit of tourists.

Société Française de Bienfaisance Tomb, St. Louis Cemetery No. 1. This whitewashed mausoleum is one of the largest structures in the cemeteries. It rises in a solid square mass to a simple pediment, above which rests a massive truncated structure bearing the name of the society. It contains a total of 70 vaults and has about it a definite air of mystery.

Dominique You's Tomb, St. Louis Cemetery No. 2. Dominique You was one of Jean Lafitte's right-hand men. He distinguished himself in the Battle of New Orleans and later settled down as a law-abiding citizen. He was supposed to lead the expedition to free Napoleon from St. Helena and bring him to New Orleans.

Tomb of Barelli, St. Louis Cemetery No. 2. This weather worn slab cut in high relief is the most graphic delineation in all the cemeteries.

At its base the strife of life is represented by the fallen and fleeing figures from the scene of an exploding ship, no doubt the manner in which Barelli met

his death. The departing soul rises above this to enter heaven and meet loved ones while the all seeing eye in a wreath of cherubs watches from above. The three cherubs to the right are playing a lyre, a harp and a flute. Note the great inverted torches, symbols of death, on either side.

Tomb of Greek Architecture, St. Louis Cemetery No. 2. This tomb, erected
when the Greek revival was beginning to sweep Louisiana, is a Greek Temple
in miniature with ornamental pediment and entablature.

Single Tier Tombs, St. Louis Cemetery No. 2. These single tier tombs, found only in St. Louis Cemetery No. 2, rise to a height of five or six vaults and are usually topped with wrought iron crosses.

"*Silent Tents*," St. Louis Cemetery No. 3. The striking similarity between this row of tombs recalls the lines from Theodore O'Hara's poem: "On fame's eternal camping ground their silent tents are spread."

Mother and Lost Child. This beautiful and pathetic little statue is found on top of a tomb in St. Louis Cemetery No. 3. Its lifelike proportions together with the expression and attitude of utter grief shown by the young mother for her lost infant make it a work of art.

This bas-relief work, topped by roses and morning glories, shows hovering angel ready to grasp the mother's hand for the ascension. Probably the mother and infant died at childbirth.

Delicate Detail in Stone shows the Sacred Heart of Christ encircled by a wreath of flowers cut in high relief. This particular stone, harder than most, has preserved all the sharpness of the stone cutter's art.

Christ's Head and the Crown of Thorns. Although overshadowed by the ironworker the sculptor has played an important part in the art work of the older cemeteries. This anguished, resigned face of the Savior is in St. Patrick's Cemetery No. 3.

Tombs Beneath the Oak. In Cypress Grove Cemetery the tombs and oven vaults are shaded by ancient live oak trees.

Oven Tombs. Along the boundary lines of the older cemeteries are walls of tombs built in tiers. These vaults, called "ovens," are rented for a certain period after which they can be opened and reused.

Scene in Cypress Grove Cemetery. The arched pediment of the central tomb shows the Roman influence and is typical of many of the older tombs. Obelisks and pylons were also used extensively. Here the blinding white tombs against the sinister background of moss draped oaks create the weird and dreamlike atmosphere found in surrealist painting.

Tomb of New Lusitanos Benevolent Association, 1858. This architectural masterpiece with crumbling walls and sprouting vegetation is in the old Girod Cemetery, the oldest Protestant burial ground in the city. The beautiful Greek doric columns, the detached pediment, the white stone slabs standing out against the darkness of the heavy metal doors, and the delicately grilled window, create a feeling of melancholy beauty and mystery.

St. Roch's Chapel, St. Roch's Cemetery. The chapel was built in 1871 by Father Thevis, a young German priest, in fulfillment of a vow that if St. Roch would help his congregation through the yellow fever epidemic of 1866-68, he would erect the chapel with his own hands. Of Gothic architecture, it is small and narrow with walls of considerable height. On each side of the interior are tombs and behind the communion rail is a large collection of crutches, false limbs, and braces left by those who have been cured.

Tomb of the Twenty Sepulchres, St. Roch's Cemetery, belongs to a German Woman's Society. These small mausoleums erected by societies are constructed with the vaults in tiers similar to the oven graves.

Tomb with Pylons, Lafayette Cemetery No. 2, was erected by a mission home. The growing vegetation is quite common on the older tombs. The Egyptian-like corner pylons are unusual.

The Swan Boat on the Audubon Park lagoon. This ride up the beautiful waterway is a great favorite with both children and grownups.

Of the city's public parks, two are outstanding. On upper St. Charles Avenue, directly across from Tulane University is the main entrance to Audubon Park, named in honor of John James Audubon, the artist, and ornithologist. Extending back to the Mississippi River, it has facilities for horseback riding, swimming, golf, tennis, baseball, and boating. In the section next to the river are an aquarium, a seal pool, and the zoological gardens.

At the end of Esplanade Avenue, the equestrian statue of General P. G. T. Beauregard, "the great Creole," stands at the main entrance to City Park Besides the usual recreational facilities, City Park has the Delgado Museum of Art, a large football stadium, and a series of beautiful lagoons for both boating and fishing.

INDEX

INDEX—*Continued*